BOOKS with X-Ray VISION
SHARKS

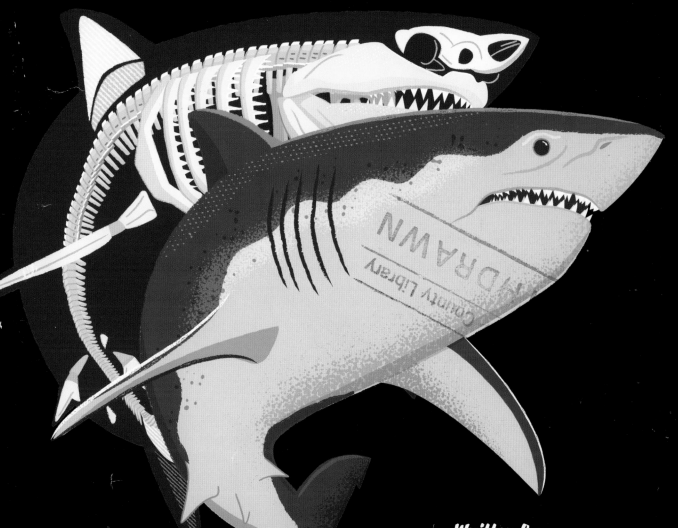

Written by
David Stewart

Illustrated by
Diego Vaisberg

Published in Great Britain in MMXXI by
Book House, an imprint of
The Salariya Book Company Ltd
25 Marlborough Place, Brighton BN1 1UB
www.salariya.com

ISBN: 978-1-913337-67-4

1 3 5 7 9 8 6 4 2

A CIP catalogue record for this book is available
from the British Library.

Printed and bound in Malta.

Visit
www.salariya.com
for our online catalogue and
free fun stuff.

PAPER FROM
SUSTAINABLE
FORESTS

Consultant: Helen Lambert is an animal welfare
scientist who is recognised around the world for
her expertise and research into animal emotions.
Helen has spent years working and researching
for the charity sector, and she now runs her own
consultancy business: Animal Welfare Consultancy.

Author: David Stewart has written many nonfiction
books for children. He lives in Brighton, England,
with his family.

Artist: Diego Vaisberg works as a designer and
illustrator. He has previously worked in the
product and design department for the Ink-co kids'
accessories brand, and has been professor of Editorial
design and Illustration at Palermo University, Buenos
Aires since 2014.

Editor: Nick Pierce

Contents

What *is* a shark?

Sharks are cold-blooded sea creatures. They have muscular, streamlined bodies and breathe through their gills. They are also very intelligent animals with large brains and good memories.

Some species of fish have rigid skeletons made of bone, but sharks' skeletons are made of a flexible material called cartilage.

Skate

A skate has a cartilage skeleton, so it is related to sharks. Skate live on the seabed and hunt crabs, lobsters and octopuses.

Shark

Sharks have rough skin without scales. Sharks' gills look like a line of slits with no covers.

X-Ray VISION

Hold the page opposite up to the light to see what's inside a shark.

What *is* inside a shark?

The shark's skeleton supports its body. It also protects the internal organs – the heart, stomach and so on. The shark's spine or backbone runs all along the body, from the cranium (skull), which protects the brain, to the tail.

Denticles

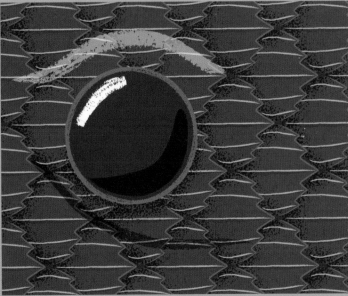

Sharks' skins are covered in denticles. The word means 'small teeth', which is what the denticles look like up close.

Gills

Sharks have five, six or seven gills on each side of their throat. Water from the shark's mouth passes over the gills. The tiny blood vessels in the gills take in oxygen from the water. Sharks breathe with gills.

How do sharks swim?

Swimming in the sea is much harder than walking on land. Most of a shark's body is made up of muscles attached to its spine. A shark's streamlined body means it can move quickly and easily through the water.

Bony fish have swim bladders to control their depth in the sea. Sharks don't have swim bladders. This means that if a shark stopped swimming, it would sink.

Did you know?

Sharks' livers are full of oil. This gives them buoyancy (the ability to float) which means they do not need to use too much energy when swimming.

Great white shark

The great white shark is a killer. It eats seals, penguins and other sharks. It has also attacked people who are swimming in the ocean. It can grow up to 6 m (20 feet) long and is very aggressive.

The torpedo-shaped body of the great white shark means it is a capable and fast swimmer. They can swim at speeds of up to 40 kph (25 mph) and can go up to 56 kph (35 mph) for short bursts of time.

Swimming movement

To swim, the muscles on one side of the shark's body contract (tighten). When the muscles on the other side do the same, it makes the shark's body bend. The shark beats its strong tail at the same time and moves through the water.

Basking shark

First dorsal fin

Second dorsal fin

Did you know?
Basking sharks swim with their mouths open to catch tiny plankton they feed on. The basking shark is the second largest living shark – adults can grow up to 8 m (26 feet) in length.

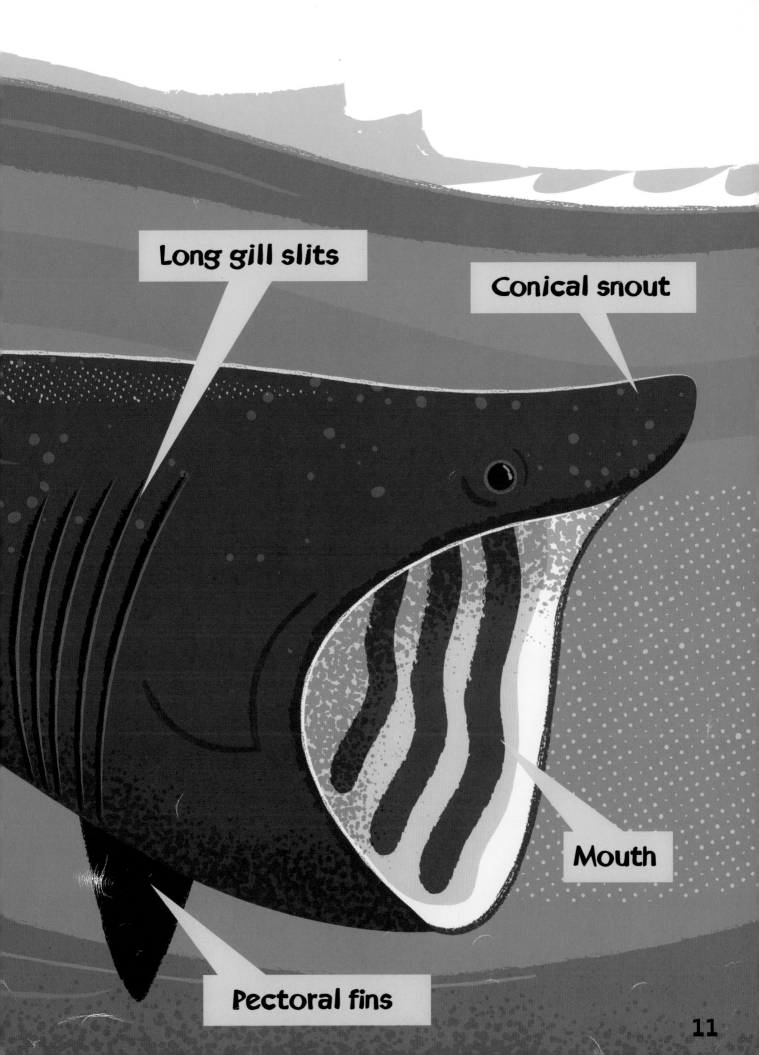

How do sharks hear and smell?

Sharks can hear, smell and see extremely well. They don't have ear lobes like people do, but a shark's hearing is probably better. The semicircular canals in a shark's ears help it to balance as it swims.

A shark's body has a row of cells along each side called the lateral line. These cells detect movement in the water near the shark.

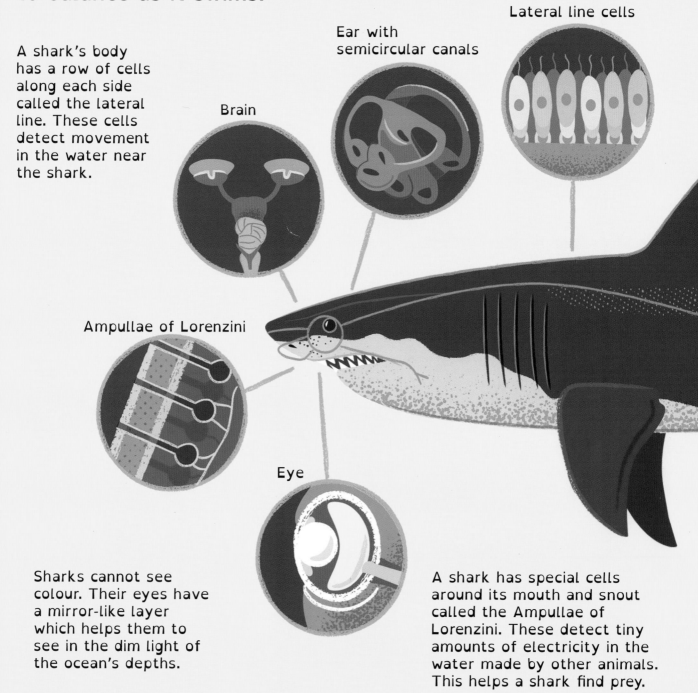

Lateral line cells

Ear with semicircular canals

Brain

Ampullae of Lorenzini

Eye

Sharks cannot see colour. Their eyes have a mirror-like layer which helps them to see in the dim light of the ocean's depths.

A shark has special cells around its mouth and snout called the Ampullae of Lorenzini. These detect tiny amounts of electricity in the water made by other animals. This helps a shark find prey.

Did you know?

A hammerhead shark's nostrils are at each end of the 'hammer' of its head. When it smells blood in both nostrils, the shark knows its prey is straight ahead, even if it's half a kilometre away.

On the underside of sharks are sensitive cells called pit organs, protected by special scales. The organs are part of the shark's well developed senses, although no one has yet discovered what they do. It is thought they allow sharks to sense water currents.

Scales covering pit organs

Different sharks' eyes show the different ways they live. Fast hunters, like the reef shark, must be streamlined and they have eyes set into the head. Rays and sharks that live near the seabed, like horn sharks, hunt by sneaking up on their prey. Their eyes stand out more.

Different eyes:

Ray

Angelshark

Reef shark

Horn shark

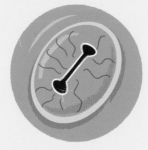

Epaulette shark

What do sharks eat?

Almost all sharks are carnivores, which means they only eat other living creatures. But what they eat depends on where they live. Mako sharks live in the Atlantic, Pacific and Indian oceans. There they catch squid and fish such as tuna and mackerel. Port Jackson sharks feed on sea urchins, shrimps and shellfish on the seabed around Australia.

Upper tooth

Lower tooth

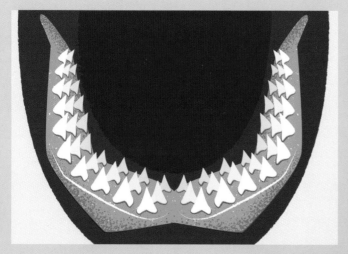

Sharks' teeth

The teeth of a shark grow in rows that slowly move outwards towards the edge of the mouth. Teeth in the outer row become worn and fall out or get pulled out when biting. They are replaced by teeth in the row behind.

Sand tiger shark

The sand tiger shark has vicious-looking teeth used for catching fish in the shallow waters of the North Atlantic. The long, sharp inward-curving teeth help it to grip its slippery prey.

14

Different teeth:

Did you know?

The thresher shark has a long top part to its tail. It thrashes the water near fish to force them into a group and stun them, which makes them easy to catch.

Sharks that eat different types of prey need different types of teeth. Long, curved teeth grip prey. Blunt teeth crunch shellfish. Jagged teeth cut through flesh.

Basking sharks and whale sharks have tiny teeth because they just gulp seawater and feed on the plankton filtered out of it.

Lemon shark

Tiger shark

Sand shark

Mako shark

Dusky shark

Bull shark

Caribbean Reef Shark

Did you know?

The Caribbean reef shark is one of the largest top predators in the reef ecosystem. They are mainly found in the Western Atlantic and off the Caribbean coast and can grow up to 10 m (33 feet) long.

Which shark is the biggest?

The two largest sharks in the world are the basking shark and the whale shark. Basking sharks grow to about 6–8 m (20–26 feet). Whale sharks usually grow to 5–10 m (16–33 feet), but some reach 18 m (59 feet). Instead of being fierce hunters like most sharks, these huge creatures eat plankton and tiny fish.

Basking shark

Dwarf lanternshark

Even when fully grown, dwarf lanternsharks are smaller than a human hand. Very little is known about this shark as they are hardly seen due to their miniature size.

Did you know?

A basking shark gulps down about 1.5 million litres (330,000 gallons) of sea water an hour. As water passes through the gill slits, the plankton are filtered out.

Plankton

Near the sea's surface it is warm and light. The millions of microscopic plants and animals that live there make up plankton. They can only be seen using a microscope.

Whale shark

Did you know?

The scuba diver beside this whale shark shows just how huge this species of shark is. Although the whale shark can swim fast if it senses danger, it normally moves quite slowly.

How do sharks hide?

Like all predators, sharks need camouflage. Tiger sharks have striped skins and leopard sharks have spotted ones so that they almost blend in with their surroundings. These sharks are difficult to see as they hunt among reefs or on the seabed.

Angelshark

Angelsharks' skin is sand-coloured to look like the sandy seabed. They eat shellfish and fish such as dabs and soles. Angelsharks get their name from the two fins they have on their backs.

Blue shark

From underneath, the pale belly of the blue shark makes it difficult to see against the light.

Did you know?

The tiger shark is as fierce a hunter in the sea as the tiger is on land. It hunts in the reefs of tropical seas, the broken stripes on its skin making it very hard for its prey to see.

Tiger shark

Lesser sandshark

The lesser sandshark's spots match the seabed, making them difficult for their prey to spot before it's too late.

Wobbegong shark

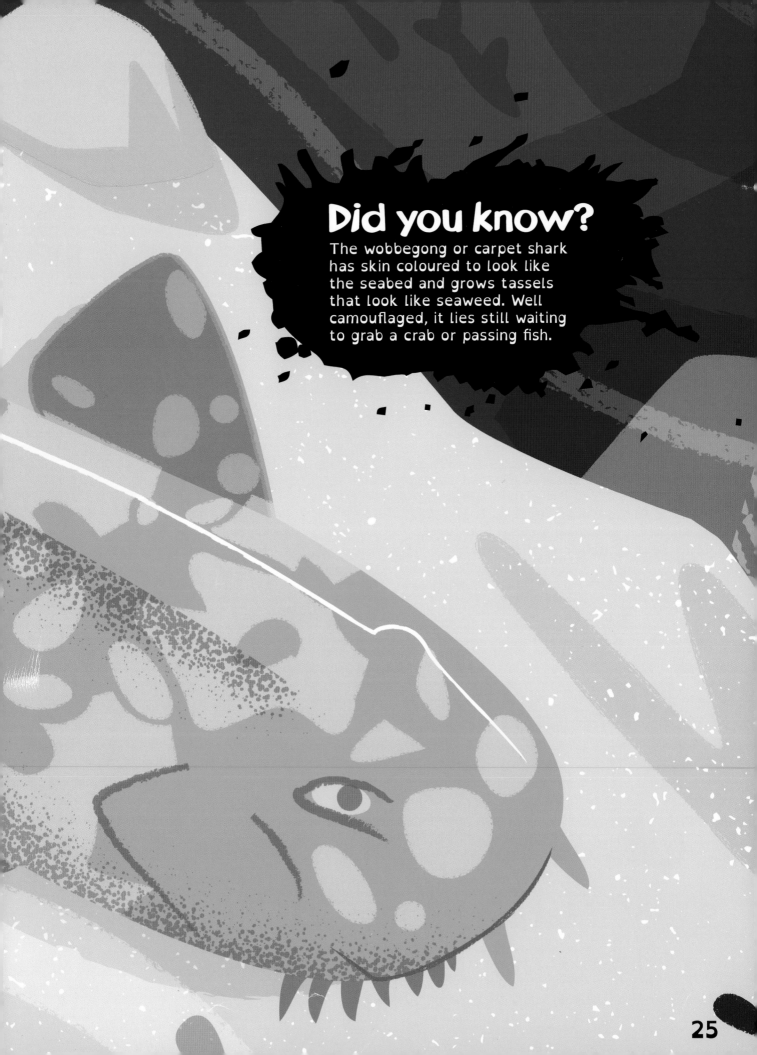

Did you know?

The wobbegong or carpet shark has skin coloured to look like the seabed and grows tassels that look like seaweed. Well camouflaged, it lies still waiting to grab a crab or passing fish.

Do sharks lay eggs?

All baby sharks are born from eggs, but not all sharks lay eggs! In many species of shark the eggs develop inside the female and she gives birth to fully formed young sharks called pups. Spurdog sharks develop inside their mother's body for between 18 and 22 months.

Port Jackson shark's egg

The female Port Jackson shark lays eggs protected in screw-shaped cases (right). She screws them into gaps in a rock for extra protection. Then, like all sharks, she swims away leaving the eggs to hatch on their own.

Mating sharks

When some sharks mate, the male holds the female with his pelvic fins and places sperm in the opening of her egg tubes.

X-Ray VISION

Hold the page opposite up to the light to see what's inside a shark.

How do baby sharks grow?

Inside each shark's egg is an embryo and a large yolk. The embryo will develop into a baby shark, or pup. The yolk is attached to the embryo and provides all the food the pup needs to grow. When the yolk is finished it is time for the pup to be born.

Newborn pups look just like small versions of adult sharks. Their parents do not look after them, so they must hunt for food themselves straight away.

The best and safest place for any baby animal to develop is inside its mother. Developing embryos only protected by egg cases or shells might be eaten or smashed against rocks by rough seas.

One-month embryo

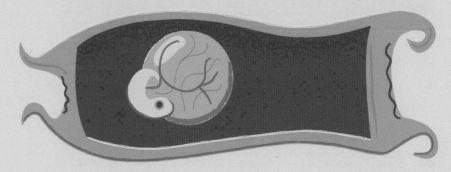

Three-month embryo

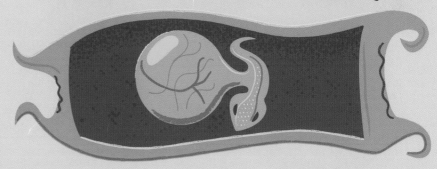

Seven-month embryo

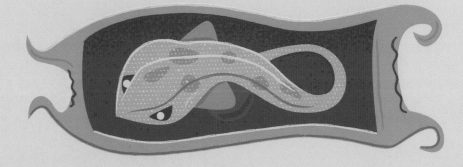

Sharks' eggs have tough, flexible cases. They often have long curly threads that become tangled in seaweed to stop them being swept away.

Where do sharks live?

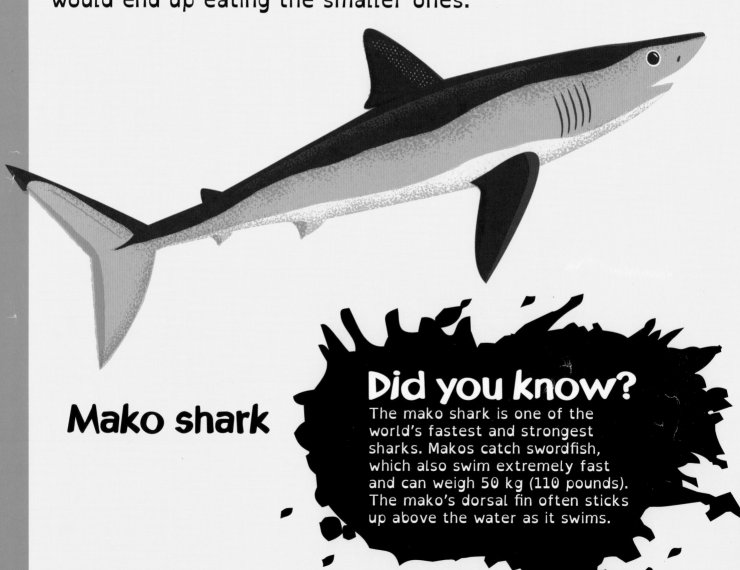

Sharks are cold-blooded, which means they cannot control their body temperature. Sharks rely on the temperature of the water around them to keep their bodies at the right temperature. When sharks live in groups, each member of the group is about the same size. If the sizes were mixed, the larger sharks would end up eating the smaller ones.

Mako shark

Did you know?

The mako shark is one of the world's fastest and strongest sharks. Makos catch swordfish, which also swim extremely fast and can weigh 50 kg (110 pounds). The mako's dorsal fin often sticks up above the water as it swims.

Lanternshark

The lanternshark lives at depths of 2,000 m (6,562 feet), where it is very dark. It gets its name from the small light organs on its belly although no one knows how it uses them.

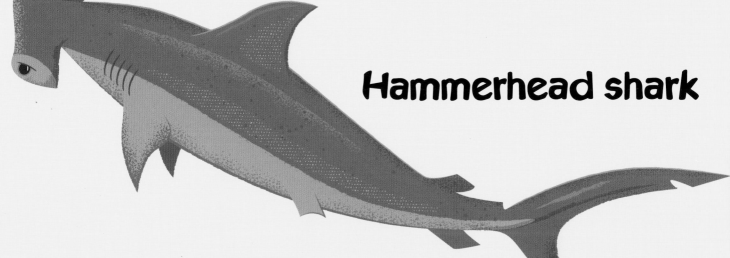

Hammerhead shark

Sharks cannot live in the Arctic or Antarctic Oceans because those areas are too cold for them. However, they can be found in all of the other oceans around the world. Many sharks are found in more than one region of the world's seas. Very few sharks can live in fresh water.

The hammerhead shark lives in tropical waters across the world and they have been known to mass migrate in the summer months to cooler waters.

Where in the world are sharks?

Pacific ocean

Atlantic ocean

Caribbean sea

Key

Dogfish shark

Basking shark

Cow shark

Hammerhead shark

Angelshark

Weasel shark

Requiem shark

Barbeled houndshark

Bamboo shark

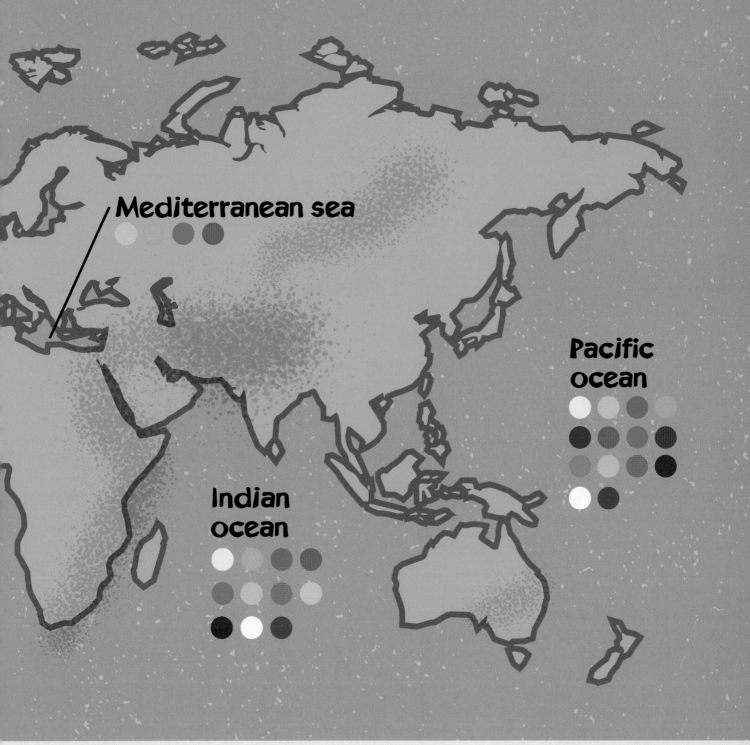

Mediterranean sea

Pacific ocean

Indian ocean

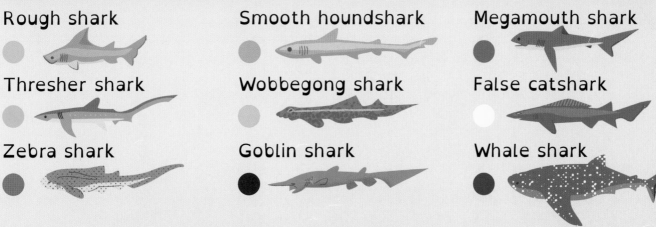

Rough shark

Smooth houndshark

Megamouth shark

Thresher shark

Wobbegong shark

False catshark

Zebra shark

Goblin shark

Whale shark

How can you see sharks?

An aquarium is probably the best place to see sharks. But keeping sharks in captivity is difficult. It is much better to see them in the wild. Some scuba diving holidays include the chance to swim with sharks.

A Jacques Cousteau diving saucer

Jacques Cousteau, the French undersea explorer, helped design this 'diving saucer' in 1959. Made of steel 2 cm (0.8 inch) thick, it let scientists observe sea life deeper underwater than ever before.

Views of the saucer from the front (above) and from the side (below).

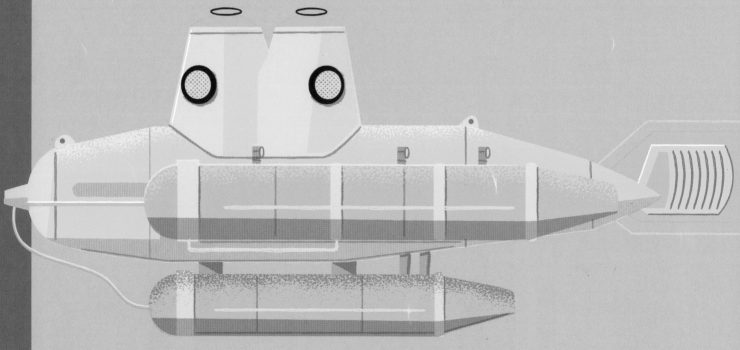

Diver's cage

This great white shark (below) is attacking the shark-proof cage protecting the diver.

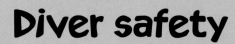

It is important for scientists to be able to get this close to sharks and be safe. This is the best way to learn as much as possible about all sharks, but many are easily scared and studying them is difficult.

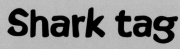

Diver safety

This diver (left) is protected by a special, tough plastic box and is quite safe as he swims up to sharks to study them.

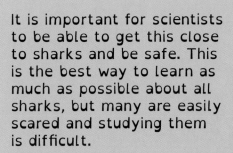

Shark tag

Scientists catch sharks with bait. Each shark is then tagged with a number and a radio transmitter so it can be tracked once it has been let back into the sea. This helps scientists to learn about the movements of the different species of shark.

Sharks in an aquarium

Did you know?

An aquarium is certainly the safest place to see sharks. You will be able to get really close-up views. But sharks need so much space that it is difficult to keep them happy and healthy in captivity.

Why are people scared of sharks?

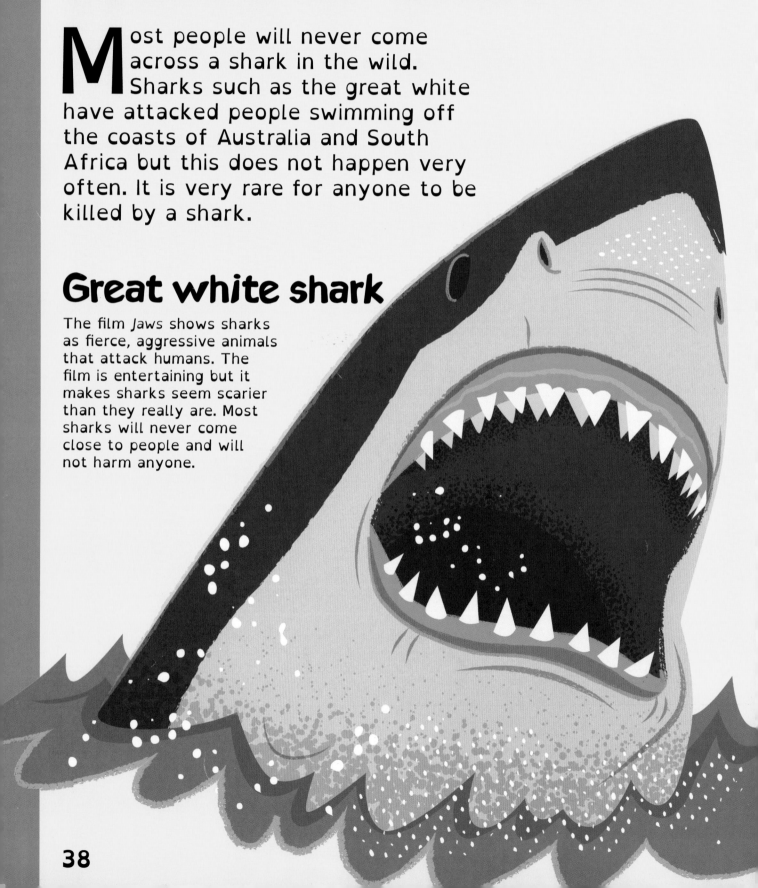

Most people will never come across a shark in the wild. Sharks such as the great white have attacked people swimming off the coasts of Australia and South Africa but this does not happen very often. It is very rare for anyone to be killed by a shark.

Great white shark

The film *Jaws* shows sharks as fierce, aggressive animals that attack humans. The film is entertaining but it makes sharks seem scarier than they really are. Most sharks will never come close to people and will not harm anyone.

Shark bait

Many species of shark live far out in the depths of the oceans so we know very little about them. That is another reason why myths about their fierceness have grown up. Some sharks will come and take bait (left), giving scientists a chance to study their jaws.

Did you know?

Blood attracts sharks quicker than anything else. The species with the best sense of smell (like the great whites) can smell blood from up to 400 km (249 miles) away. That's equivalent to one drop of blood in a small swimming pool. Not all species can do this though.

Protective explosives

Did you know?

Jabs at their eyes and gills will sometimes frighten away sharks that come too close. Divers likely to meet the great white shark, nicknamed 'white death', often carry a stick with them. It has an explosive on one end in case they are attacked.

Hammerhead shark

Did you know?

Each year thousands of sharks die tangled up in fishing nets or caught in defence nets near swimming beaches. Most of these sharks would never have gone near a human, let alone attacked one.

Why are sharks killed?

Sharks are killed for many reasons. They are caught for their flesh, which is eaten or made into fertiliser. The oil from their livers is used in medicines and make-up. Sharks are also killed for sport. Some species of shark have been hunted so much they are now in danger of becoming extinct.

Tooth necklace

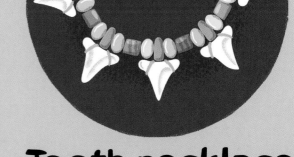

Some tourist souvenirs are made of sharks' teeth, like this necklace (above). If people stop buying them, then perhaps fewer sharks would be killed to supply the trade. Hunting and killing something for pleasure seems pointless when all you have left of a magnificent creature is its jaws to hang on your wall (left).

Shark jaws

Shark skin

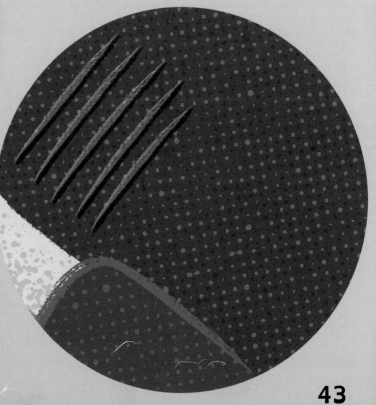

Sharks are sometimes killed for their skin. It can be made into fine bags and wallets and people pay high prices for it. A shark's skin is so rough that it has previously been used to smooth and polish things. This material is called shagreen.

Why are sharks important?

Sharks are apex predators that play a vital part in the ocean's ecosystem. They sit at the top of the food chain and without them the entire balance of marine life would be disrupted. Many countries rely on sharks as a means of tourism. If humans continue to kill sharks for pleasure or personal gain, they will destroy our oceans too.

Shark diving

Shark diving is a growing industry, which attracts tourists each year. This benefits both the tourism company and local communities, as people come to stay and eat in their businesses.

The food chain

Quaternary consumers

Without sharks to keep the numbers of smaller predators in check, fish up and down the food chain will be affected. Humans will also be affected as there will be no fish to catch for food.

Without sharks, the population of smaller hunters will increase. More fish may sound like a good thing but an increase of smaller hunters will mean the number of reef fish will decrease.

Reef fish feed on coral reef, which prevents it becoming overgrown with algae. If that happened the coral reef would die and there would be no safe place for fish to breed and lay eggs.

Tertiary consumers

Secondary consumers

Primary consumers

Primary producers

Did you know?

The presence of sharks in our world has shaped marine life and its ecosystems for more than 450 million years.

Shark facts

Female sharks have thicker skin than male sharks. This is to protect them from the males if they become aggressive during the breeding season.

The female sand tiger shark usually gives birth to only one pup at a time. This is because the one pup has eaten any others that were growing inside its mother!

Young basking sharks are about 1.5 m (5 feet) long when they hatch.

The huge whale shark can feed upright. It rises to the surface, then sinks tail first, gulping in water and the plankton it contains, as it goes down.

In 1976 sailors on an American ship found something caught on the anchor. It was an entirely new species of shark. It was named the megamouth and was 4.5 m (14.8 feet) long.

The cookiecutter shark's teeth are so strong that it can bite holes in the rubber which is used to coat submarines.

More than 400 species of shark live in the seas and oceans around the world.

The fossilised teeth of a mako shark have been found. They are still as sharp as when it had its last meal about 75 million years ago!

Port Jackson sharks are also called pig sharks. They have large, downward-pointing nostrils that look like a pig's nose. The shark uses them to sniff out its prey on the seabed.

Fossils that have been found show that sharks were swimming in the Earth's seas and oceans 450 million years ago.

Cladoselache, the oldest known shark, was 2 m (6.6 feet) long. Because sharks do not have skeletons of bone, the only shark fossils are their teeth. The rest of the cartilage skeleton rots away completely.

One ancient shark, Otodus megalodon, had teeth about 11 cm (4.3 inch) wide and 15 cm (6 inch) long. The great white shark has teeth 3 cm (1 inch) wide and less than 4 cm (1.6 inch) long! Otodus megalodon probably weighed about 50 tonnes (55 tons). It became extinct 3.6 million years ago.

Rock salmon is another name for the dogfish, a small species of shark. Rock salmon and chips is eaten in Britain.

Glossary

Aggressive Something which shows fierceness.

Camouflage A colouring or shape which helps an animal blend in with its surroundings.

Cartilage The flexible, gristle-like material that sharks' skeletons are made from.

Cold-blooded An animal whose body temperature changes according to the temperature of its surroundings.

Cranium The part of the skull that protects the brain.

Denticles The small tooth-like growths that cover a shark's body.

Embryo An unborn creature that is developing either in its mother's womb or inside an egg.

Extinct Species of animals that are no longer alive anywhere in the world.

Fossil The very old remains of a plant or animal.

Gills The organs that sharks and fish use to breathe.

Microscopic Something so tiny it can only be seen under a microscope, not with the naked eye.

Plankton The microscopic plants and animals that live near the surface of the sea.

Predator An animal that hunts other living creatures for food.

Prey Animals that are hunted by other animals for food.

Quaternary consumer Predators who eat a lot of prey without being eaten themselves.

Species A group of living things that share at least one feature and can breed together.

Streamlined Something that is able to move easily through air or water.

Swim bladder An air-filled sac that bony fish use to control their depth when swimming.

Tertiary consumer An animal that eats primary and secondary consumers.

Index